HARPER-ARRINGTON
P U B L I S H I N G

The Reality Of Owning and Operating Your Own Clothing Line.

Special Notice: If you purchased this book and the cover is missing or the cover does not match the one on our website – please contact us immediately at 888-435-9235.

Harper-Arrington Publishing
18701 Grandriver Ave.
Suite 105
Detroit, MI 48223
T: 888-435-9234
F: 248-281-0373
Website: www.startingaclothingline.com
Email: info@startingaclothingline.com

Edited By Marc D. Baldwin, PhD

Printed in the United States of America

Disclaimer:

This manual is for your general reference on starting a clothing line. We have taken every step to ensure that all the information presented here is accurate. We are not lawyers and therefore we are not contending to give you any legal advice. We give you suggestions to follow at your own will. We cannot be held liable for any of the information presented in this book. You are completely responsible for any decisions that you make.

Submitting Your Review of this Title

We are very interested in knowing what you thought of this manual. Please send in your review to reviews@startingaclothingline.com. Your feedback and thoughts are very much appreciated.

Titles currently available from Harper Arrington:

Please note that all three of our manuals work together to make up our full course on starting your own clothing line and being successful at running it.

  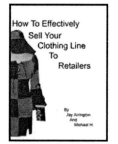

Volume 1   Volume 2   Sales Guide

All three books are available along with other fashion titles and resources at

startingaclothingline.com

TABLE OF CONTENTS

Introduction

This manual was written to inform aspiring designers about the various aspects of owning and operating their own clothing line. Many problems will arise in the clothing design business that may not be your fault. Nevertheless, you will have to solve them nonetheless, in the very best way you can. In this manual we will discuss the types of problems you will encounter. We will also give you many suggestions for solving them.

We had to refrain from mentioning any brand names specifically in this book due to confidentiality. Nevertheless, we will share with you some of the experiences of other brand designers, as well as experiences of our own. You will be able to learn from the experiences referenced in this book to better prepare yourself for the hurdles of this industry. We are not authors giving you a generalized gloss over of the industry; we actually take you on the front lines of the battle to succeed.

ABOUT THE AUTHORS

The two authors of this manual are leading young designers currently operating and designing a national clothing line. The authors have been fortunate to personally experience the key points of the clothing industry firsthand. They know what it is like to start a line from scratch to actually have products in stores.

To date, the authors have had some of their pieces worn by celebrity figures. They have been truly dedicated to the fashion industry since their entry. Their passion for designing has been appreciated by customers all around the world.

Words from Michael H.

Many people start out wanting to create clothing lines from humble beginnings. Others start out on top of the world like the Sean John Label, which is one of Macy's top selling lines. No matter where you start, the fundamentals are the same. You must create a good product and sell it at a profit to make it. In this business, sometimes that is easier said than done.

This manual is the first of its kind to give you an in-depth look at the industry before you make huge financial commitments. The knowledge that is shared here will empower you. Nothing about this industry is easy; it is hard work and you have to be willing to do what it takes to make it. Just reading this manual proves you are serious about going after your clothing business dream.

Words from Jay Arrington

Give yourself an Edge

In life as in business, I work to give myself an edge over the competition and circumstances. My sincere desire is to encourage you to do the same. When we first started in the fashion industry, we strived to learn everything that we could, and to be as knowledgeable as possible.

I think it is safe to say that we've learned a lot, and now this information is being passed on to you. Enjoy it, and make an opportunity for yourself in this $90 billion industry. After all, "you can if you think you can, and if you think you can't, you're right." I read these words one day and they have stuck with me every since. You can succeed - just believe you can! Best of luck to you in your pursuit to be the next hot designer!

Building the Proper Team pt. 2
Harmony and Cohesion

A good team is essential to the success of your clothing line. Whether your team is made up of owners, investors or other talented people, it is essential that you have harmony and cohesion. It is essential that you take the needed steps to maintain the cohesiveness of your team.

There are certain attributes that are paramount to the survival of any company or organization. These attributes are respect, professionalism, and integrity. In order to provide optimal performance, each team member must maintain these characteristics.

Without these three attributes, internal problems could take place and compromise the foundation that you are building upon. For example, if someone on your team takes a leadership position on a project, and the team agrees that he/she is making the right decisions, support should come from the other members of the group.

What I just stated might seem obvious, but many nascent companies have failed before they could really get started. In plain English, internal arguing among team members slows down or may destroy your progress all together. If you want to be successful at starting any company, there must be harmony and cohesion among the team members at all times.

Now I'm not saying you should strive to make your company a utopia. In reality your team *will* have disagreements. Nevertheless, there is a way to disagree professionally without caving in your entire company. Unity within the team will be a key to your success and it will be the team's responsibility to maintain it.

One method we use to help maintain unity on our team is called "The We Factor." "The We Factor" is when the team works as a unit and no longer as a collection of individuals. The language of the team also changes from "I did" to "we did," and every move one person makes for the good of the team is considered a move for us all.

This way of doing business will eliminate finger pointing when a team member makes a blunder or mistake. The team should agree as a whole before any moves are made. It is at this point that a change in language takes place and you begin to say "We" instead of "I."

This industry is full of ups and downs and setbacks. Our aim is to give you as much insight into this industry as possible and prepare you for the road ahead. Since our team has traveled this road before, our hindsight can serve as your foresight.

A very important thing to remember is to always expect the unexpected; unforeseen problems are notorious, relentless and bound to happen. The team's job is to anticipate and try to problem solve any problems before they occur. Remember anything that can go wrong will go wrong. So whatever task you are performing, ask yourself what can go wrong. Then be prepared if what you imagine actually happens. You will be better prepared to handle the good and the bad when you have a supported team.

There is no I in the word TEAM; **T**ogether **E**veryone **A**chieves **M**ore.

Designing Your Collection

Designing your collections is one of the fun things about this business. For many reasons you may be actually producing only 25 percent of the things you really like. One factor that influences how many designs you will bring out is financing. Your budget - the factory minimums - may only allow you to produce so many styles per month or season.

For example, say you only had $1,000 and one style was costing you $10 each. The factory said that you had to order at least 100 per style. You would only be able to produce that one style. To a designer, not being able to bring out all of your designs can be frustrating.

You may find yourself having to alter your designs if you can't fit them into your production schedule when you would like to. You may also find yourself having to change the fabric of certain styles. If your fabric choice is important to the design, then you may have to wait until that season comes back around next year to make that particular style.

By the time that season comes next year you have other designs that probably will come before that one. Next thing you know, you may have to totally scrap the original idea or incorporate certain aspects of its' design into newer styles.

Another aspect of designing your collection is fabrication and coloring. It is important when you are designing to know what factory is going to make what styles and when. Suppose you have a pair of denim jeans that have suede on them. The suede on the jeans is supposed to match up with the knit sweater being made by a different manufacturer. This is a bad idea.

It is very hard to have two separate manufacturers match up the same color, even if using pantone reference as you learned in Volume I. There was a time we didn't consider this. One particular order we did could have turned into disaster. We received samples from that order from each manufacturer about a week apart. On paper the designs were looking great. However, once we saw the actual samples together, we knew we had a problem with color matching. What you have to remember is that many times you don't see what the actual fabric color will be until months into the production phase.

Sure, you will see lab dips, but these don't give you the full understanding as seeing the entire garment in its chosen color does. We had a model try the clothes on from that order and it was terrible. The colors did not match whatsoever. Here is a rule you should always live by: when you are doing a bottom that is supposed to match with a certain top, color for color, make sure the two colors don't touch. There should be a contrasting color separating them.

It is our practice and that of other clothing brands to have multiple manufacturers on the roster. No one relies on just one place to do everything. You have to have back up plans and be well diversified in your production allocation. Say you are working with just one manufacturer and things go wrong, which they often do for various reasons. Then your designs will have no manufacturing home, and your pipeline is delayed.

The pipeline is an important factor to the clothing entrepreneur. Without a strong pipeline, you will not be able to compete with the competition or keep your cash flowing. The pipeline simply refers to the number of styles you are releasing in sequence (by date).

For an exercise: Go to the mall once a week and count how many times you see something new - something that you didn't see before from a particular brand. How long did it take before you saw those new items? In general most companies bring out new styles once a month. If you are not bringing out new styles regularly - at least once a month - then your clothing will look old on the rack compared to the just arrived styles from your competitors.

The Pipeline

So when designing, you have to make sure you have strong styling in your pipeline. Each release should be hotter than the last. The last thing you want is your March delivery styles to be hit and miss with buyers after your February styles were too hot to keep on the racks. You have to be consistent in releasing hot styles. You don't want to end up being a one hit wonder.

The next thing about the pipeline depends on your factory. You have to make sure you have your production orders in place to be able to keep your pipeline intact. Once again new designers don't really think about this area. It has a lot to do with budget forecasting and timing. Timing is one of the most important elements to a clothing line. It is not like selling soap where it doesn't matter when you get it into your warehouse and begin selling it.

Now to further this, let's do a skeleton example of a pipeline plan. Say you have an order of jeans coming in January. You have an order of skirts coming in February. You have an order of jogging suits coming in March. Now, to be able to guarantee that each of these orders will arrive on time, you have to do your part.

Your part is either to issue a LC or place a down payment on the order to get it in motion. So, say each of these orders is going to cost $15,000 FOB (FOB term from Volume 1). If you were to sell out of your January order in thirty days, you would have the money you invested in the order back - plus profit - in February theoretically.

In order to have a January order in the first place, you would have had to order it the previous October or even September. You would have started your February release in the previous October or September. You ordered your March release in the previous November, your April release in the previous December, your May release in January. By the time you order your June release, you would have the money from your January order back to invest in June's Production.

If you chose to pay a down payment to your manufacturers, the balance payment to them might not be due until two weeks before they ship your order out. Now if you are having your goods flown by air delivery, then the date of two weeks prior to your January order falls on December 15. If you were using ocean shipping, then you would have had to pay your balance sometime the previous November.

Let's assume that you are paying 50 percent down on your order when you place it. We also assume in this example that your company's first income is not coming until February. Assume all you have in financial resources at this time is your initial investment money.

- January - $15,000 you have to pay out of your investment.
- February - $15,000 you have to pay out of your investment.
- March - $15,000 you have to pay out of your investment.
- April - $7,500 down payment out of your investment.
- May - $7,500 down payment out of your investment.
- June - you don't have to pay for this order out of your investment money. You could wait until the money comes in from your January order to place a $7,500 (50 percent) down payment on the order.

In this example, you need a total of $60,000 for your production, in addition to shipping and duty costs. You would not have to pay for shipping cost until the goods arrive at your port. Therefore, in this example you only have to cover your January and February shipping and duty expenses prior to your first profit earnings.

There is a catch, however. If you get this expenditure schedule rolling from the beginning, you will be in somewhat good shape providing you pay everything on time and your manufacturer ships everything on time. The catch is that you have to sell out before your next production payment is due, or you will have to borrow to cover it in this example.

Donald Trump said that having a hot product may come easy but selling it is the hard part. You have to sell your merchandise for this equation to work. If you don't, your pipeline is in jeopardy. Now what happens when you miss a month in your pipeline? One result is that the profits from the current order you have on the table must now fund your expenses and production for the next month. Your financial burden on previous profits picks up when you have a non-released or late orders.

Example of a well flowing pipeline:

- February you have made $30,000 from your January order

- You have expenditures of $10,000 (salary, loan payments, advertising, office expenses, etc.)

- You put $7,500 on your June down payment

- You pay the shipping for your March or April order depending on your shipping method. Say it is $3,000 for this example.

- You now have $9,500 left and you will be adding your March profits to that.

Example of a poorly flowing pipeline:

- February you have made $30,000 from your January order

- You have expenditures of $10,000 (salary, loan payments, advertising, office expenses, etc.)

- You put $7,500 on your June down payment

- You pay the shipping for your March or April order depending on your shipping method. Say it is $3,000 for this example.

- You now have $9,500 left

- Your March order has been delayed to April because the manufacturer is shipping to you late.

- Now you have to take that $9,500

- Put down $7,500 to keep your pipeline running

- You only have $2,000 left for expenditures and shipping cost of March. You would be $8,000 short in this example.

- What do you do? Borrow? Do you not put down the deposit?

- Your other bills and commitments are due.

Now if you don't sell out within thirty days prior to your next month's delivery, you will run short even more money. If you are running short already and your delivery is late, you could start seeing a month or two go by without a new product in your warehouse.

When the pipeline fails, your designs have to either be altered or cancelled. This is the nature of the beast. You may be thinking, "what if I just try to come out with a new product every other month?" Depending on your overhead and your expansion plan, this will cost just as much money as coming out with something new every month.

The other thing to keep in mind with your designs is that stores like variety. They want to see a wide array of clothing. Therefore, you as a designer can't go into their showroom with just one pair of jeans and one shirt. The other side of that is you can go into a retailer meeting with four different styled jeans and four tops and the retailer will just order one style. The business is crazy that way.

The best thing to do is present a big line on paper. You can have a catalog full of different styles. You know that you are only bringing out so many of them; meaning you already placed a factory order for a select few. If they order any style that you aren't bringing out, tell them that particular style is not available right now. This channels them to the styles that you are bringing out.

If you find that most stores always want the things you aren't bringing out, then you should reconsider how you are deciding what designs to put into production. Remember, this plan will only work if your pipeline is going smoothly and you are delivering to your retailers on time. If you are not then you have more problems to contend with. Not only will retailers become fed up if they can't get certain styles that they really want, but their second choices are arriving to their stores late.

Aren't these things good to know? You will hear these things only in our book. We will repeat this point throughout the book to help you understand precisely why it was worth your investment to have this manual.

Now on to your truly large companies like Tommy Hilfiger. They order their clothes nine to twelve months in advance of their street date. This means that their designs for 2006 are mostly finished in early 2005. These companies are so large that they have to operate in this manner to ensure factories can make their orders on time.

You have an advantage because you can get your product to the market faster than the big boys. Moreover, if you are air shipping, you can get them out even faster. You can actually design something today and have it out in 90 to 120 days on average. Use this advantage wisely. Think of it this way. If the Tommy Hilfiger Company forecasted a trend that didn't materialize, it is in trouble. Your ideas by contrast should be right on the money because you have the advantage of seeing new trends first hand and react on them.

With all of this being said, if you were a large brand, you would need quite a bit of money to start up and run your operations. Imagine if your production orders per month were $300,000 or more. Our example above is based on a spending budget of $15,000 a month on production.

Assume you have to order 500 of every style you order. Suppose each pair of jeans you order will cost you $12 FOB and each top will cost $9 FOB.

500 pair of style 1: = $6,000

500 tops of style 1: = $4,500

Your total for this one complete outfit is $10,500.

If you only had $15,000 to put toward production that month then you could not get two outfits. Say that you didn't have a separate budget for your shipping and duty, then your $4,500 will be gone as well. Among the 500 that you are ordering, try to get the manufacturer to give you at least two colors, meaning 250 of color 1 and 250 of color 2. Do not be tempted to increase your quantity because you may have $4,500 left if you don't have orders for that additional product. As we talked about in Volume 1, it is better to sell out and not have enough than to have more than enough.

What make designs cost what they do to be produced?

- The amount you order

- The price of the fabric per yard

- Cutting and Sewing

- Dyeing cost

- Washing cost

- Trims

- Packing method

As we all know, the more we buy, the cheaper the price gets. Remember that it is better to have an empty warehouse because you sold out of a product that you paid $5 for rather than a warehouse full with leftover merchandise for which you only paid $3. Getting your money out of excess inventory can be very tough.

The price of the fabric per yard is also a factor in the unit cost of your styles. If you make your goods with cheap fabric then your goods will be cheap goods. Consumers can spot a cheap fabric a mile away. Also note that factories have certain minimums of yardage that they have to order or make per run. This will also determine the number of pieces of a certain style you are required to buy.

Factories in China are very good to suggest using Ramie Denim for your denim styles. Why is that? We will tell you. Once again, you will only hear this here as we give you the real world insight. Chinese manufacturers will offer you a pair of Ramie Denim jeans for a unit cost of, say, $6. Sounds like a good price, right? Ramie Denim is cheap. If you are making a low cost denim brand then Ramie Denim is for you.

Ramie Denim is a quota-free fabric. Chinese manufacturers try to push this fabric off on new clients because it saves them money and hassle in quota cost and stipulations. We have had a few manufacturers try to sell us on Ramie Denim, but guess what? We turned them down each time. We know that Ramie Denim is a cheap fabric that would not represent the upscale nature of our line. Go out to your local mall and see if any other company in your market is using Ramie Denim.

Cutting and sewing is one of the most expensive parts to manufacturing your garments. The more pattern pieces you have in your style, the more it will cost. This is why complicated styles cost more money to make. Make sure that within your market you can get your money out of a complicated style. You have to be able to obtain a reasonable profit margin off each style. You can get a good mark-up without too much backlash from retailers if you have a hot and in-demand clothing line.

Dyeing also makes up a part of your unit cost. Factories have to dye certain amounts of fabric at one time. It is in your best interests to use **the same fabric in a number of different styles**. Factories will like this as well. This also is a benefit to your collection. Say you want two different styles of tops. Say the factory tells you that you will have to order 500 of each. You could ask the factory if it can produce 250 of each style since both styles use the same fabric. A manufacturer may go for this.

In the reality of selling your product, it is better to have two different styles of tops in the same color than to have just one style top done in two colors. Another thing to keep in mind about dyeing is maintaining color consistency. If you order 500 tops of the same fabric, make sure you tell the factory to order enough fabric plus additional yardage (cover factory mistakes) to make sure they can dye all 500 units at the same time. Fabric in this case would all be of the same dye lot.

One time we ordered 450 dresses. The factory actually screwed up on 125 dresses, so they scrapped them. They then brought in some more fabric to remake the 125 dresses. The problem with this was we had a dress and hat set. When the dresses came in, some were the original color and some were the color of the second dyeing. We had to match up the hats and dresses before we shipped them because of the color difference.

Your trim cost is often minimal. Trims are mostly labels and hang tags. The greatest expense in producing trims is setup cost. For instance, you will have to pay a mold charge for each trim you have made. You will be charged for your button designs, rivets, custom zippers, and so on. Most factories will charge you up front for this.

You can opt to have the unit cost per trim included in your FOB cost per style or you can buy the trims in bulk. It is up to you and your manufacturer. Your reason for paying up front may be to save you money in the long run. You can actually have all or some of the trims shipped to you directly. The trims will come in handy as you can send them to any new manufacturers to be used in your samples.

Sometimes relationships go sour with manufacturers. You may find that you can't get the bulk trims you paid for without other stipulations. In these cases, you will have to invest in mold charges all over again with a new manufacturer. It is good to get any excess trims you paid for sent to you before any full production order is actually done. Of course leave your manufacturer with what they need and some excess to cover any mistakes during production.

Packaging your orders is not that expensive. You stipulate how you want your goods packed, as learned in volume 1, and go for it.

We will tell you about a incidence that happened to a company we know. This story will help you understand why you need exposure to the fundamentals of this business before you can be successful. Having hot designs does not guarantee success. There was a guy who was a hell of a designer. He worked for a major brand designing some of their most signature pieces. For whatever reason, he decided that he wanted to leave the company.

He started his own company a short time later. Now remember, this person was hot with his designs. Retailers jumped on his product because of the buzz he had coming from this major label. He picked up industry sales representatives because of the hype that pushed his product. Coming out the gate, his product was initially purchased by over 250 stores. Despite his enviable early success, this man is no longer in business just one and a half years later.

Why is he out of business? Being a good designer doesn't necessarily make you a good businessperson. Now what exactly happened in this case? This is a lesson to learn from. It involves something we talked about earlier, which is the great big **Pipeline**.

Now as we told you, this person came out of the gate with over 250 stores calling for his product. He only had a certain amount of money to finance his collection for the season and spent it in a way that did not protect his pipeline. Suppose you had $1,000,000 in your bank. You bring out clothes once per season, which is every three months. Retailers bought heavily into this man's season one releases, to the tune of $2,000,000 in sales. To keep things simple, assume his markup is double. That means his production cost on $2,000,000 in sales would be $1,000,000.

These are guaranteed sales. What do you do? Do you realize that you need to split that $1,000,000 into being able to fund at least three seasons (securing your pipeline) and loose money (short-term loss) on all of the orders placed with you, or do you strive to accommodate the orders? This man chose to go after his orders. Now what is wrong with this, you might ask? He should be able to use the $2,000,000 he will make to keep things going, right?

This theory did not work for this man and it will not for you either. Whether your line has millions to spend or thousands, the issue of time management comes into play. For those of you looking at this, as I don't have a million to spend anyway, think again. The reason why is because of the amount of time it takes you to get your next product from the sample stage to a finished product in your warehouse.

A number of things went wrong for this person. First, his product did not sell in the stores as everyone thought it would, despite his designs being hot. No one can say what exactly will be a hit with consumers. His product did do well in a lot of stores. However, consider this: many of his retail accounts were done on credit.

He shipped his product to stores on January 1. He had ordered the product in September and so spent his whole $1,000,000 dollars in September. He had no money left to spend in October for products that would have come out in February etc. Now in February, he had less than the $2,000,000 he had sold because some accounts simply did not pay on time or at all. The accounts that did well, meanwhile, were asking him what he had coming out the following month. Nothing at all, he had to respond. His pipeline was empty. As February and March rolled in, his hype had begun to diminish. His accounts had started to move on.

Don't make this mistake. It is better to sell out by not having enough than having too much. Also note the fact that because he didn't totally sell out in thirty days or even within that season, further set him up for doom. Now, let's apply this man's difficult experience to a smaller scale.

When we first started our line we made this same mistake. We had just run a production run of 250 jogging suits out of China for $38 FOB each. The joggings suits sold out, as they were one of the first of their kind. We decided to re-design the outfit and release it again because all of the success we had. We found a factory in Korea that could do the jogging suits for $22 but we had to order 750 sets. Selling the remixed suits for the same price meant we could make far more money off the deal.

We timed things so that when we started making money off the jogging suits, we could pay our final payment to factory for the next order. Two problems arose. The first one was that the jogging suits were a month late so we didn't have the money to pay for the next order on time. This delayed the factory in finishing that order. When our new jogging suits did come in, we picked up extra freight cost, as expected. Even though the FOB price was lower, we still paid more in total duty cost because of the quantity.

We had to sell at least 400 suits to break even and pay for the next order. It took us forty-five days to do this and collect our money. This further delayed our next order. By that time, our next order was already two months behind the jogging suits, which meant that all of the other orders in our pipeline were affected. Now if we had just ordered another 250 or even 400 jogging suits at our old cost, we would have sold out and been able to keep things rolling on time.

Time is money. If you try to finance your company with one product of which you order a lot of, you will have difficulty in the long run. You have to build slowly, diversify, and grow. Ordering one product in bulk would work if you could have your clothes made, shipped, and sold out in thirty days. Unfortunately things don't turn that fast in the fashion industry.

I want to give you one more example to drive this lesson home. Say you invested your whole $25,000 investment in one order because you projected that you could make $75,000 off it. Say you are selling this to retailers and directly to consumers. First, when retailers allocate a certain amount of space in their store for your line, and give you a piece of their budget, it is yours. It is yours until you no longer make them money. Now if you give them your product in January, they have put your line into their budget.

When February comes, you don't have a new product for them. The money they had for you will be spent on someone else's line. What if that new line sells at a faster rate than your line does? What if your line produced just average sales in their store? They may have been willing to give you another shot in February but you aren't bringing anything out. Now your spot is gone and you will have to re-earn it. This is not always easy.

Now say you have your revenue of $75,000 in February. You are in the same position all over again but with a little more money. Do you invest in one production order or fill your pipeline? Hopefully you know now that your pipeline comes first. For another example, think about the following case. Say you have a $2,000 check that you were going to buy a car with but you just were laid off. That $2,000 will be your last check for three months. Out of that $2,000, you have to pay bills until you go back to work.

By the time you figure out what your monthly overhead is and other expenses, you may find you only have $1,000 or less left for that new car after three months. The same principle applies here. Your $75,000 could erode to $40,000 or less after four months of waiting to get your new order in. This is even assuming that you actually make the full $75,000.

Financing Your Line

Financing your line can be stressful. We covered some ways in Volume 1 to get it done. There is no one way of finding financing. We will not cover traditional bank financing, as it doesn't exist too much for the garment design company. As learned in Volume 1, having orders or hot designs doesn't automatically mean that someone will be willing to loan you large sums of money.

As we stated in Volume 1, the best source of financing will begin with you and the assets you can pull together. The next level of financing is seeking small and large investors. Suppose you knew ten people who each could loan you $5,000. Having a great business plan, attractive samples to show, orders, and a great repayment plan may be all you need to land some small to large size capital investors.

Try to pool together as many small investors as you can if you can't find one person with a large amount to invest in you or to borrow from. We use the term investor loosely here. Look at investors as two types. You have your short-term investor and your long-term investor. Short-term investors ask for an attractive interest rate for borrowing their money. You may opt to pay them back anywhere from a month to two years later if you set up your agreement that way. Your long-term investor may be with you for the life of your company unless you buy them out or they decide they want out.

Picking up long-term investors can be good and bad. The good part is it should be a nice boost to your operating capital. You may be able to finance your production and advertising with it. Of course most investors who invest large amounts will want a percentage of your company. Give them percentages that you are comfortable with based on the amount of their investment.

The thing to keep in mind is that as with most companies, you will have a few rounds of borrowing. For instance, you may have started your company with a small amount of borrowed funds just to get started. Then you will need to borrow again sometimes to get to the next level. After things are going well, you may have to borrow again to expand your line. Now what would happen if you let somebody buy into your company with $10,000 and you gave them 10 percent during your first round? Say you had three people like that. That is 30 percent of your company gone already.

Then in the second round, say you found an investor who has $100,000. Even though a $100,000 isn't a lot of money in this industry, say they wanted 20 percent for their investment. Now you would have 50 percent of your company gone already and all you have to show for it is $130,000.

If your line begins picking up at a fast pace, you may need to expand beyond the current profits that you are making. Then you would need a third round of borrowing. Keep in mind that most companies have many rounds of borrowing. Now if you bring on one more investor, you should be seeking a minimum of $500,000 or higher at this point. This investor will want a percentage of your company too. What do you do? Well, you could try to buy out the other investors, but this will cost you. Otherwise, you stand to lose controlling interest in your company.

Our advice is this: borrow smartly. Your plan should be to go as far as you can on your own finances, as mentioned in Volume 1. Next you should seek smaller investors to whom you will pay back their money within a specified period. Smaller investors are people with less than $15,000. Next you have your $50,000 to $100,000 type investors.

$50,000 can be spent in one month just financing one or two orders or meeting advertising costs. After that $50,000 is gone, you better be selling your merchandise to be able to maintain your company.

Therefore, in reality, you should try to come up with at least $100,000 through small investments. If someone did want to invest $100,000 or more, you should think about giving them around 5 to 15 percent. Make sure you have planned on how to put your investments to efficient use. You should not allocate all of your investment funds at once. You should save some as patch money.

Patch money is funds you can use if your sales are going slow or you have a gap in your pipeline. This is kind of like a nest egg in a sense. They say most businesses fail because they don't have enough capital to make their cash flow smoothly. This is true. This is why we say you need to save a portion of your investment funds to ensure that your cash flow and pipeline stay in good shape. As a rule of thumb, you always want to invest the bulk of your money in what will make you money.

Bringing in large investors is a good thing, but realize that the more people who invest, the more control or input they will want. There is a clothing line that we know of that went to the Magic Tradeshow that had a small booth at first. They later got new financing from a larger (non-apparel) company.

They returned to Magic with a larger booth the following season. They were able to step up their image and begin doing national advertising. The investor began calling most of the shots. This brand did not take off as the designers or the investor wanted it to. The investor pulled out, leaving the company in a position where they could not go on. In this case, their failure was mostly due to poor advertising and a bad name to begin with, among other things.

The same concept happened with another somewhat famous urban line that had a major rapper attached to it. The designer was able to get financing from a larger clothing brand because the line was doing so well. Once the line stopped performing, the larger clothing brand pulled out, leaving the company high and dry. The larger company did not care about the company attempting to make a comeback.

The moral of this story is once you get a large investor, you had better make sure you take your company to the top and stay there. Should that investor pull out, it could mean the end of your company. You would be forced to start over. The problem is that retailers took a chance on you once and they might not be willing to do it again.

Reading this book places you in the position to know what to do with your investments. To be quite honest, you should not start your business officially until you can at least secure $100,000. This means that you should not spend any of your investment money until you have reached this amount. Trying to make a run at it with less than $100,000 is possible but hard.

Keep in mind that the early legwork mentioned in Volume 1, such as getting your office together, trademarks, and the cost of your first round of samples, should be done out of your pocket or with credit cards. Be creative in how you come up with your financing. Just remember who you get in bed with - bedfellows can be good things, but also very bad things. Make smart moves. Always think of long term objectives. Do not keep your mind in this moment alone. You don't want to end up owing large sums of money to investors that you can't pay back.

Manufacturing

Manufacturing is one of the most complicated pieces of the puzzle. Manufacturing will either make you or break you. There is much to be said in this section. In reality, this is the life or death section of this book. Right now you should be extremely glad you purchased this book.

We will start at the beginning. As you learned in Volume 1, it is best to only seek manufacturers after having a good understanding of how the whole process works. To everyone we state buyer beware when sourcing your garments to overseas factories! Unless you stay on top of your production, you may end up with something different from what you were expecting.

Before doing business with an overseas manufacturer, put that manufacturer through the initial contact verification check. Check out all of their contact information as learned in Vol. 1. Then begin a series of e-mail trading to get a full understanding of what they can or can't do. Don't be fooled by manufacturers telling you how great they are on quality. Many will tell you about all of these processes for inspection and being ISO 9001 certified. These claims may be true but don't place too much weight upon them. We learned some claims are just plain old lies the hard way.

The bottom line is you are never really guaranteed quality unless you watch your product being made directly. If you were to spot something wrong, you would tell the manufacturer to fix it right then and there. If you don't have the means to do this, then your chances of receiving the quality you want are **never 100 percent**. There are times when things will go beautifully and others when your product will resemble the curbside on garbage day.

In this section, we will explore some various quality issues that happened to us and some of our colleagues. Our first production run went pretty good. We worked with a manufacturer out of Hong Kong. At the time they were doing work for another well-known brand. Hong Kong in general is one of the most expensive countries to do work in except for manufacturing done in Europe. At the same time, Hong Kong gets high marks on quality.

We worked with one Hong Kong manufacturer for about four or five orders. The problem came with our sixth order. Since we had been working with the company for a while, we asked them to help us get a denim maker who could do small quantities. We ordered some men's denim jeans and denim tops. Once manufactured, however, the buttons began to fall off the pants and tops. How could something as simple as putting on buttons be done wrong? We couldn't blame this whole thing on the Hong Kong business because they had actually sourced our denim program to another company in China. The Hong Kong company was strictly a knit company. However, all financial dealings on the order still went through the main Hong Kong company.

In this particular order, we purchased one garment style top and one garment style jean bottom that both came in three colors. The black color had its share of problems, which was totally unexpected. The denim of the black outfits had a strong smell, like Kerosene. It was terrible. Who would imagine that your garments would not arrive odor free? Really, is that something you should have to worry about? Yes, everything becomes important when you are sourcing your goods from overseas, or from anywhere for that matter. To be honest with you, we probably could write a whole book on overseas manufacturing. You even have to specify with manufacturers that your garments should be free of any soiling or stains.

Anyway, the third problem with this order was the indigo color. We had suede on these garments and if the garments were washed, the indigo would bleed on the suede. The catch to this was we asked the manufacturer to do a dry clean test on the garments before they shipped them. All the tags were dry clean only. Their test came back possible. However, when we put the garments in the cleaners here in the U.S., the garments failed miserably. Consequently, we had to offer a lot of refunds, credits, and replacement outfits to satisfy customers.

The final blow with this order was that we were force into producing a color scheme that we really didn't like. The blue and red style we had was one of the weakest colors of the three. We had originally set up to do two different styles that would use the blue and red color. We canceled one of the styles and wanted to take the money from the canceled style and add it to the indigo color. The manufacturer would not let us, and then force us into getting more of the blue and red style.

This was poor planning on our part for changing the styles up in the middle of the order. We were left on the short end of the stick. We had too much of our weakest color. When we sold these items to the stores, the black and the indigo colors sold out which left us with blue and red outfits. It was a blow to our cash flow because now we had a certain amount of dollars we were expecting to make held up in this style.

What you have to remember is that if you are counting on bringing in a certain amount of money from an order and you don't get it, you will have to make cuts in other areas. We next shifted our production to India. We took our production to India because the U.S. dollar is worth a lot of money there which makes their production pretty cheap. Unfortunately, we got what we paid for. India's manufacturing proved to be very disappointing. Now if you look at some well-known labels, you may find some with a "made in India" tag from time to time. These tags are found primarily on tops and T-shirts. Don't make denim jeans in India. Trust us.

One of our accounts always talks about another designer who was doing production in India. I remember the storeowner said you can't go too far when you have your clothing made in India. I was thinking to myself, "that may be true but we are working with a good guy over there." I was so wrong. When our denim shorts came in, they were the worst.

Loose threads were hanging everywhere. The buttons were banged up pretty bad and were not highly polished, as they should have been. Sure, we had seen the production samples prior to shipping and honestly they looked good. There are times you will receive a nicely constructed sample and then your production looks like garbage. The grading was even off on this production run. There were some good pieces out of this order. We did manage to sell the good ones, but not at the price we originally intended to sell them for.

Basically, we are trying to make you aware of different aspects that will need your attention when doing overseas production. Now, on that same India order the tops had problems. We had a very nice quality T-shirt. In fact, India is known for their great cotton. The fabric was absolutely wonderful. The main problem that affected every piece was that the front neck drop was too low and the width too wide.

The larger sizes were affected the most by this problem. The smaller sizes could pass. The other problem was that the printed logo on some shirts was not straight. It was slanted in some cases. Imagine how that looked! Yes, this was truly a bad order.

One of our colleagues at the time moved his production to the country of Pakistan. The prices were good and the manufacturing agent was doing some work for another company he knew. For those of you who don't know what a manufacturing agent is, we will tell you. A manufacturing agent is an intermediary between you and the factory.

The manufacturing agent is the one who will quarterback your deal to manufacturers with whom he or she already has a relationship. This is supposed to guarantee you quality and delivery etc. Agents charge you a fee for their services. Usually this fee is a percentage of each unit price multiplied by the total quantity ordered.

Most of the time the agent fee is already included in your unit cost. We have always paid directly to the agent in these cases. The agent then forwards the money to the factory when it has finished production and done work to meet your standards. A manufacturing agent is supposed to be your safeguard.

This is not always the case, however. Think of this scenario that happened to our colleague's line. A problem arose during the manufacturing of one of our colleague's styles. This style was very important to our colleague's company because he had advertised it everywhere. The buzz for it was crazy. The product was severely delayed. The agent turned out to be a very shady liar.

If an agent or company keeps offering you excuses as to why your product is running late, and the delay goes beyond two weeks, they maybe trying to stall you. This agent was saying things like he was waiting on labels to come in from China. Our colleague said I can't wait for that. Do it without those particular labels. The agent would say things like, no you paid me to do a job for you and I want it to be just as you ordered it. At first our colleague thought, "ok this guy really cares." Yeah sure he did! This was a stalling technique. If this kind of talk persists in your own agent relations, you will have to perceive the negative pattern and call your agent's bluff.

The next stall technique the agent used was that he claimed that the production had actually finished, but the manufacturer was having problems getting the order on a plane to the U.S.A. He stated that there was severe backlog and delays at the airport. He went on with this lie for three weeks. Can you believe that? Our colleague was calling over there every night trying to figure out what was really going on.

Our colleague called in a different freight broker to get the goods out of Pakistan. The new freight broker stated that there was no holdup in shipping out of Pakistan. This was a shocking blow to our colleague. He was furious over the fact that this agent had been lying now for two months. Attempts to get the agent on the phone were proving to be unsuccessful. The agent was avoiding our colleague's calls.

Then the final bomb dropped on this particular order. The agent had finally realized that he could lie no more, as our colleague had now discovered the truth. He apologized and said that he wanted to tell the truth but couldn't let our colleague down.

What actually happened is that the agent, without notice to our colleague, had switched factories from where he normally gets production done. He had never worked with this new factory. Now keep in mind that our colleague had a signed contract with the first factory. Being that our colleague was not informed of the factory change; the new company had no contractual obligations to our colleague to adhere to any delivery or quality standards.

The new factory took their sweet time filling the order. At the same time, the new factory did not really care for the agent. It was a bad situation in which our colleague's company had to pretty much sit back and wait while his extremely advertised style slipped away. This is an extreme case of poor manufacturing but we have to include it. You have to be prepared for anything with overseas manufactures.

A manufacturer delivering your products late is a big problem. The first thing is to make sure you have done your part to ensure that your order gets started on time. If you know you need an order to come out by Christmas, you have to order it no later than August. Next, you need to make sure you are completely satisfied with the styling of whatever it is that you are ordering. Last minute changes by you will further delay your order.

Manufacturers hate last minute changes, but it is the way of the business. Don't let them tell you that it is not. We once had a manufacturer tell us that last minute change is somewhat a norm. However, major last minute changes will cost you more money and delay your order. Simple changes can be knocked out sometimes without missing a beat. Keep in mind that some manufacturers may stop working with you if you become notorious for last minute changes on orders.

There was one time when a last minute find in our production sample saved us. We were making some women velour jogging sets on this particular order with another company from Korea. We had just received the samples in and the ship date was the next day. As we brought in models to try the clothes on, we noticed there was too much material in the hip area.

It was a huge defect.

We immediately got on the phone and e-mailed the manufacturer as well to stop them from sending this order. It is hard to imagine what we would have done with a defective order at that point once it was on U.S. soil. Paying for reworking once the goods arrived in the U.S. would have forced us to sell the items for more than the market would allow. The company ended up reworking the order in Korea because it was their fault. They were still not happy about doing it; they would have rather we hadn't caught their mistake. Where was their so-called quality check at that point?

The bad part is this order was supposed to come in early November but ended up arriving two days before Christmas. The good thing is the order turned out to be very successful for us in terms of the fit and sales. The women really loved the jogging set and it sold out in all of our stores. Don't be afraid to stop an order when you find something wrong with it at the last minute. You may lose time, but this is better than losing time *and* money.

After you have ensured that you have done your part to get your order finished on time, it is completely up to the factory from that point. When you place an order with a factory, they will look at where in their production schedule they can fit you in. In general, they try to knock out their most profitable production clients with the big orders first, then squeeze in lower volume orders.

Sometime a manufacturer will give you a completion date without really having any real intentions of meeting that delivery date. You will have to stay on the manufacturer and enforce any late penalties that you have agreed upon in your manufacturing agreement. Don't be scared to enforce this contract. You will want to have some of the following stipulations in your contract with your manufacturer:

- If they don't deliver by a certain date, they will be held financially responsible for any changes you have to make to the styles, which could include new fabric, changing the style, etc.
- Your reason for the above stipulation is that you are missing your season and now can't sell the order as is.
- Keep in mind this may further delay your order.

Now the bad part of this is you may get a discount off your late order but you are the only one who will really suffer, as we mentioned above when discussing the pipeline. Now your January order has turned into your February order. Your February order has turned into your March order. Now you have to review all of your styles and make sure they are still season appropriate for their new dates.

In some cases, you will end up having to alter your styles or cancel them. Meanwhile, your profits are not flowing because of the delay. Your retailers are mad because you aren't delivering on time. As we said, they don't care that the factory made you late; being late only reflects on you and your company in their eyes.

In our beginnings, some five years ago, we were caught up like this. We went to the Magic Tradeshow in Las Vegas and wrote $110,000 in orders. We went to an August show and wrote orders for our immediate items and our future delivery items. We shipped our immediate items but our future delivery items ended up being delayed. Our pipeline was not where it should have been. Why do you think we are strong advocates of the pipeline now?

We wrote $70,000 in future delivery items that never saw the light of day. A delay here, lack of money there, and so on gradually wiped out our paper pipeline. We lost all of those orders for those items. Manufacturing delivery time is critical to your success. It is your job to stay on the manufacturer to make sure they do your order on time. They should be on time with each manufacturing milestone in an order as outlined in Volume I. This will ensure they are at least making progress towards the completion of your order.

In reality you should make the manufacturer feel that they are lucky to be working with you. You have to possess the power over them. You have to make them do what it is you want them to. They will take advantage of you if you don't. In our early days, we were taken advantage of a lot. We were fortunate enough to keep things going, but it was not easy at that time. We could have easily fallen off our track and failed.

Now back to quality. Quality is the number one reason why you and your manufacturer may part ways. It is a beautiful thing when a sample comes in looking like garbage. Then you know right then and there that it is time to head for the border. The unfortunate thing is when samples come back looking good, and turns out to be essentially a front to get your trust.

Manufacturers know how to trick you. Many of them offer you false promises of excellent manufacturing but can't deliver. There was a company we worked with in Bangladesh. They sent us beautiful samples and production samples. Based on the production samples, we paid our balance to them and asked them to ship our product.

When the product came in, we were totally taken for a long ride. They had changed the fabric on us to a cheaper fabric and our suede trim was definitely not suede. To make matters worst, the grading was so bad that our size ten, twelve, and fourteen all fitted like a size eight. We could not sell this product at all. We had to pull it from all of our catalogs and orders. It was a disgrace.

We had written in our contract with the company that if more than 20 percent of an order was defective, we would have to be reimbursed or credited the full FOB value of the order plus any shipping and duty expenses we paid. Guess what? They never paid us a dime. This is an unfortunate part of wire transactions when paying factories. If this had been on a LC (Volume 1), we may have had some real recourse.

The last major thing of this nature to happen to us was when we ordered some different jogging suits out of Korea. A colleague recommended this agent to us. We felt the agent must be pretty good if our friend's company was using her. The bad part is we had a chance to let another company do the manufacturing but chose the Korean woman instead based on our colleague's referral, even though she was $2 higher per unit than this other factory.

The jogging suits were a disaster. The zippers were falling off as soon as you tried to zip them up. This affected about 50 percent of the order. The grading done on the jackets was off to the point where we had to substitute jacket and pants sizes just to make it work. For instance we had to sell an XL jacket with a large pair of pants, even though it was suppose to be a matching set.

When you are getting your production samples in you need to do the following:

- Request to see each size you ordered

- Request to see each color you ordered

- Make them confirm that the samples are from the actual production lot.

- Inspect them thoroughly

- Make sure the garments are free of strange odors

- Pull on the zippers

- Pull on the buttons

- Wear them to make sure the fit is right

- Measure them to make sure the fit is right

- Put them in the washer, dryer, cleaners or whatever you have on your care label

- Make sure decorative designs aren't crooked on the garment

- Make sure nothing is missing

- Make sure the stitching is straight

- Make sure there are no broken stitches

- Make sure stitching is neat

- Make sure your pockets are deep enough or not too deep

- Make sure your pocket openings are the right size

- Make sure the labels are correct

- Make sure the colors on your hangtags are not bleeding on your garments inside the polybags

- Make sure they are using quality dyes, and that the dyes are fully setting into your garments

As far as measurements are concerned, they must be within the tolerance you specify. The spec handbook we recommended to you in Volume 1 will help you to understand the meaning of tolerance. It will also give you standard industry tolerance levels for certain styles.

You will want to do all of these checks to whatever sample you receive from your manufacturers. It is extremely important to do these checks on the production samples. The last thing you need is to get defective garments into your warehouse. These checks do not guarantee that there will not be any bad apples in your mix, but it does give you a little peace of mind.

Now your product is ready to ship. You have set up your account and terms with your customs broker etc. The manufacturer is supposed to send a Visa with the shipment to get it cleared once it reaches your country. Make sure they have filled out the Visa information correctly before they ship your goods. They must have their garment category numbers correct for your styles (see Volume 1).

We have suffered delays four times over visa issues. Two times, our visa was lost. Once the visa was sent directly with the shipment and then lost by the airlines. The other time we had decided to send the visa by Federal Express to our broker. Even so, the Visa arrived after the order by a couple of days which still slowed us down. Two other times there were mistakes on the visa.

When a visa is incorrect or lost, you should expect a delay of at least a week before you can get a new one. In the meantime, your goods are sitting in an airport warehouse gaining storage fees. If you want, you could tell the manufacturer that if the visa is incorrect because of an issue on their end, they will be responsible for excess storage fees while you are waiting on a new visa.

Next, you have to get your goods through customs. The people at customs work strictly by the book, which is a good thing. You should always plan for delays through customs. If for any reason you need to contact customs about your order, your customs broker may be your only means of communication with them.

We once had a customs agent who wanted to know what method was used to sandblast our jeans. As it turns out, some company has a patented process for doing sandblasting. We had to tell customs that we were not using that particular method. It was quite interesting. At the time of writing this book, who wasn't sandblasting? Is customs asking everybody this question? Who knows?

To close this section, we want to emphasize the following points. Many new designers think that once they have a manufacturer who is willing to work with them, the sky is the limit. Relationships with many manufacturers are like one night stands. It is hard to find a good manufacturer who you can work with for the long term. When you do have one, be sure to do your part to keep your relationship in good standing.

As they say in relationships, the grass is not always greener on the other side. The other point here is to make sure you have the manufacturer sign off on your terms and provisions. Remember from Volume I that even the conditions of the boxes they ship your clothes in are fair game for stipulations.

You have to be the boss. In our company we always assigned one person to be really friendly with them. We had another person who would be on them about things they were not doing correctly. have to know that your company is serious.

In order for the manufacturer to know this, you have to know how to deal with them. You have to be precise in your decisions and objectives for your brand. You have to know what you are doing. Unfortunately, many times new designers rush to get manufacturing and simply don't know exactly how things should go or shouldn't. Be glad you are reading this book.

Companies like T.J. Maxx and other discount chains buy defective goods and overstocked merchandise from clothing companies all the time. They buy them very cheap, so don't expect to make money there. You may end up only getting $6 or less for a product you invested $12 in. This is why it is very important for you not to over order as well. If you have too much product that you can't move, you may not be able to get the full face value out of it.

You will have to search around through various manufacturers to find one that will make the quantities you are comfortable with. Don't be afraid to be creative in coming up with how you negotiate with them on this. Many factories will tell you right in the beginning that their minimum quantity is one hundred dozens or 1200 pieces per style or more. Some of the larger factories may have minimums of 100,000 pieces per style. If that is something you can do then you are ok. If not, don't be afraid to counter them with what you want to do. It may work sometimes.

You may be able to get a manufacturer, who normally states that their turnaround is ninety days after sample approval, to make your goods in sixty days. Once again, they may say ok but still finish your order in ninety days. Good manufacturing can be achieved. It is not impossible. For every horror story, there are twice as many quality orders being delivered. Just make sure you do your part to ensure that your company gets the best treatment.

Keep this in mind as well when sourcing your production. You will want to make sure your overseas manufacturer is not a sweatshop and does not employ children. You don't want that coming back to haunt you like the Kathy Lee case. For the record, Kathy Lee is a celebrity whose clothing line took a lot of bad press because it was discovered that some of her clothing was being made in sweatshops.

Stay in daily contact with your manufacturer(s). Continually offer any help they need. Be sure that you believe them to be trustworthy before you begin basing all or part of your pipeline on them. Imagine basing your pipeline on one manufacturer who ends up going astray. Your pipeline would be wiped out while you try to bring someone else up to speed.

It is best to have a different factory working on each delivery. For instance, if you had an order coming out in January,

February and March, you should have a separate manufacturer for each of them. Then on your April order, go back to the January factory. This will ensure that your pipeline is protected. Remember these three key points:

- Protect the pipeline

- Protect your quality

- Protect your delivery date

Good luck.

The Inside Story on Dealing with Retailers

Selling to retailers in most cases is the lifeline of your company. Without proper distribution, clothing companies would not have an outlet to sell their merchandise. Sure, there are web sales, but they are a fraction of what takes place in the physical world. Most people would rather try their clothes on in stores before purchasing them over the internet.

With this being the case, you need retailers. In our sales guide, we went into the basic dealings with retailers. In this book we will actually take you inside selling to retailers. We will give you some different cases to learn from. Knowing these things will better prepare you to make sound moves when selling your line to retailers.

The first thing we want to touch upon is something we mentioned in volume 1 and the sales guide. Do not give credit to a retailer if your factoring bank doesn't approve them for credit. I remember when we first had the thought to get a factor - we were very excited. We saw getting a factor as a way to increase the likelihood that a store would order from us because everyone likes credit right? A retailer wouldn't mind having thirty days go by before they have to pay you. In that amount of time they could have sold your merchandise and let it pay for itself. The problem is many of your mom and pop type stores don't have good credit. I recall when we first got our first round of orders from Magic. We submitted all of the retailer's names that ordered from us to our factor. Out of forty stores, only three of them were approved for credit.

Some of these stores we thought were doing pretty well. However, looks can be deceiving. This business is based on image. You can look flawless on the outside but your inner workings may be deteriorating. The funny thing is some of these retailers who were not approved insisted that other factors were giving them credit. They may even insist something is wrong with your factor. For the most part, these retailers are paying COD for their orders but are trying to convince you otherwise.

We believe COD to be the best payment method if done correctly. Note: you should never accept a company or personal check for payment despite the storeowner telling you their checks are good. Don't let a storeowner talk you into accepting these forms of payment. Yes, it might be inconvenient for them to get a money order but it will be even more inconvenient for you to monitor your collections efforts on their account because they skipped out on paying you.

One of our stores at one point convinced the Fed Ex driver to let him pay for our order with a company check. Our accounting staff was upset when a company check appeared. It just so happened that in this case the check cleared our bank with no problem. That is one of the few times, however, when personal or company checks worked in our favor.

We had a store in Louisiana that was very successful. All of the hot brands were retailed from this store. Before we knew exactly how to structure the COD forms, this guy had sent us our first lesson. He paid with a company check. It bounced. He requested us to redeposit it on a certain date. It bounced again. We sent him to collections because months went by with no cash from this man, though he continued to claim that he would take care of his costs.

Another person in Pennsylvania had a similar story. He had actually been approved by the factor for $1,000 on net thirty. However, our first order with him totaled $2,000. In being new, we decided to give him the credit ourselves since he was already approved by the factor for half the amount of the order. He actually sold out of our order within two weeks and wanted to reorder.

We were excited, but at the same time we asked him to go ahead and pay for this second order COD and include the payment for the first order. It totaled up to be $3800.00. This happened at the same time as the other bad COD order in Louisiana. We did not put the proper COD secure funds labels on the package so he was able to pay with a company check.

His check bounced. We had to send him to collections. His store would later file for bankruptcy. This person actually had a history of preying upon new lines. He was notorious for writing bad checks for clothing. He tried to come off as a nice big shot in the industry. He would use the sales from new lines to pay for his other existing lines.

The moral of this story is you being the new person on the block with an unproven track record, may produce people who want to take advantage of you. Say a retailer sells $500 dollars worth of your clothes and none of his Tommy Hilfiger. The bills arrives. He may choose to pay Hilfiger over your account even though it was you who made him the money. This is very sad but it happens.

The same thing can be said of COD. Retailers sometimes have many COD orders coming in on the same day or week. Based on their funds that day or week, they may opt to pay for their most profitable lines first. Yours in this case, may not be one of them as you are new. The unfortunate thing is sometimes your package is returned to you after multiple attempts to deliver to that store are unsuccessful.

Returned packages cost you money. In our beginnings, we incurred huge Fed Ex bills. We were trying to get our money as fast as we could so we were shipping to some of our retailers using three-day express instead of ground transportation.

The reason we worked this way was for cash flow purposes. Let us break it down for you because unless you have been doing it, you will not know. Here is the general cycle.

Cash Flow In the Apparel Industry by Average Number of Days.

Start Order Downpayment	Finish Production Pay Balance	Ship Goods Air	Ship Goods Ocean	Clear Customs	Time to ship goods into your warehouse	You ship to Retailers	COD delivery to you	Bank Clear Money Order
	60	7	40	4	1	5	7	5

Total Time by Air:	89
Total Time by Ocean:	122

Looking at the numbers above gives you a general idea about how things go. We will come back to this chart in the cash flow section. Right now we want to bring your attention to the time it takes for you to ship to retailers and actually get your money order cleared at the bank.

We were sending packages to retailers three-day express because the COD check would come back the next business day. We wanted our money fast. Therefore, if a retailer would get their order the first day it arrived at their store, we would have our check the next day. This cut our time by eight days. Eight days may not seem like a lot but when you have other orders in your pipeline where the balances must be paid prior to ship can make eight days plenty.

The other way we tried to save time was to give discounts to retailers who paid by postal money order. Postal Money Orders clear the bank the same day, so you save four days on bank clearing. This is good for us as clothing companies but retailers hate going to the post office to get a money order.

That year we spent over $40,000 with Fed Ex. We learned a lesson from this. Often times we found that some retailers did not have the money to cover our orders the first time we sent them. They would then request that we resend the orders. Most of them would get the orders on the second attempt, but some still didn't get them. It is these types of retailers that you have to look out for.

The ones who eventually pay for the order have to pay for the first delivery as well. The ones who don't pay at all leave you having to cover the cost. Keep in mind that we were not actually charging retailers full shipping cost because we were shipping three-day express. Do not ship in any form but ground is our advice. Think profits over a few days saved in delivering and processing time.

We basically were throwing money down the drain in an attempt to better our order start to payment time. This one company we know of had it very bad. They had over 200 stores at one point. Many of their retailers did not pay them whether it was COD or factored money. The clothing line went out of business, owing over $200,000 to their factor and $30,000 to their freight carrier.

In this business, there will be times when you are left holding the shipping bag. It happens. The key is to not ship someone the second time without requiring that they pay up front. We had also started a plan where they would have to go get a money order first and fax us a copy of it before we shipped them. When your line is in-demand, you are in a better position to make retailers play by your rules.

Here are some of the typical excuses retailers give as to why they didn't get your package when it was initially delivered:

- They weren't at the store when it came

- They came too early

- They came too late

- They didn't have time to go out and get the money order

- They couldn't leave the store to go get the money order

- They didn't have it at the time because they got so many other COD orders that day or week

- They say things have been slow

- Can you resend it on this date?

- They had the wrong amount made out

- They simply forgot

The funny thing about sending COD is this. You always want to call and verify with the store right before you ship their order. You want to tell them the amount and what day it will most likely reach their store. They will say, "ok, send the order." If you're dealing with an unreliable vendor, four days later the package is coming back to you with one of the excuses above. It's like, "hey we just talked to you four days ago and you said you were ready to get it."

This business is crazy like that sometimes. It happens to all clothing companies that send COD orders. This is one reason we stopped doing COD to direct mail order customers (non-retailers). We started making them pay up front before we shipped them. The worst thing is when your carrier commits the error of not enforcing the secure funds payment guarantee and a company check slips in. This has happened to us four times costing us $5,000 in lost sales. **Make sure that you insure your packages for more than the $100 that is provided automatically.**

If your carrier makes a mistake like that and the retailer gets your merchandise with a bogus check, you can hold your carrier responsible. When sending COD, here are some of the actions you should take:

- Confirm the amount with the retailer before sending.
- Give them a heads up as to when they should expect the package.
- Make sure you have designated secure funds payments on the labeling. Confirm with your carrier that you are doing it right to avoid mistakes.
- Send your packages using ground services (no overnights unless the retailer prepaid or paid you with a credit card).

- Track your shipments everyday over the internet.

- If while tracking you see "recipient not available or funds not ready" on a return slip, call that particular retailer to see what the problem is.

In general things go smoothly with retailers. If a retailer gets by without paying you, sometimes you will not be able to collect his or her money. Collection agencies are a joke unfortunately. We have sent many stores to collections over non-payment. We have never been able to collect a dime unless the store really wanted to pay us. Most of the time, you will just end up writing it off on your taxes as a bad debt.

Another potential problem happens when the retailer doesn't pay the factor. The factor has already advanced you most of the money on the sale. Depending on your arrangement with the factor, the factor could force you to repay the amount he or she advanced you. You may find that the payment you were counting on coming in from another company has now been pulled back in by the factor to cover the other guy who defaulted on his payment to you.

Another thing you want to make sure of is that when your retailers pay the factor, they indicate that the payment is for your company. There was a time when the factor credited one of our payments to another clothing company by mistake. Then the factor told us we had committed fraud because the retailer paid us directly and he had paid us as well for the same order. Then the factor withheld a $1200 payment to us to cover the advance.

We knew we hadn't committed any fraud. We called the retailer and they stated they had paid the factor back. They provided us with the check number and we called the factor. The factor found out it was his error. So we asked, "where is our money that you guys are holding?" Unfortunately for us, our factoring bank was on its' way out of business and took our $1200 right along with him. The lesson here is to verify and stay on top of everything. There are many potential problems in this business. Never become to lazy to keep everything documented.

The real issue in terms of dealing with retailers is your company's positioning. If your company is strong and in-demand, retailers are more likely to take care of you. You have to do what it takes to make your line hot. If the people are demanding your line then retailers will have to play fair with you in most cases. However, selling out in a store a few times does not guarantee they won't ever jerk you around with payments.

Department Stores

Most of this discussion has been geared toward your smaller non-chain retailers. Dealing with chains and department stores is another thing. It is every designer's dream to be sold in department stores. You should be at the top of your game before entering into such deals when they present themselves. You only get one opportunity. Make it count.

Before presenting your line to department store buyers, you should make sure you are doing these things:

- You are shipping on time (at least eight consecutive months of on time shipping).

- Your pipeline is running smoothly.

- You have forecasted your styles to the point where you know what you are bringing out nine to twelve months from now.

- You are confident based on your delivery track record that each style will be coming out.

- Your advertising and marketing has created a significant demand for your products.

- Your profit margins on each unit sold are adequate.

- You have a track record of quality manufacturing.

- You have great fitting clothes.

- You have a factor.

If you are just starting out, chances are you don't yet have all of these things under your belt. You need all of these items in place. **ALL!** You do not want to get into a department store and be right back out of the door because you rushed in. Positioning is everything in this business. If you are not positioned correctly, you will suffer various consequences.

We have seen many lines go into department stores and leave right back out with the next season. Even celebrity lines aren't exempt from this painful result. Department stores give you a certain amount of space and that space is supposed to make a certain amount of money no matter what designer occupies it. If your clothing is not selling at a good rate or at all, your merchandise will be returned to you.

Unlike with mom and pop stores, which have to keep your merchandise after they pay, department stores operate totally differently. If a significant amount of your merchandise doesn't sell, they will charge the clothing back to you, or deeply discount their payments to you. We know of one woman's line where the department store discounted her clothing to the point where she made no money at all. Also note that typically department stores typically want payment terms anywhere from net 60 - 120 days.

Now is it really worth being in Macy's if you are actually losing money? If you believe this business is about ego you should think again. This industry is about your bottom line. If you make 500 outfits and gave 250 of them to Macy's where you weren't making any money, you will go out of business eventually if you persist with this logic. The bottom line is you have to be able to generate demand. **He who has the people has the power.** It is a battle for respect in this business no matter what size of retailer you are dealing with.

Another thing to note is department stores are cut throats on your unit prices. They will try to get your product for the best price they can. Their price may be lower than your budget can take. Of course, if your line is in demand you will have more leverage when negotiating prices with department stores.

There is the belief that you can take not making top dollar for your clothing because you will make it up in the end by doing larger volumes. Now if you are producing 100,000 plus of each of your designs then this may work for you. If you are doing 1,000 of each style, under pricing your merchandise will send you packing your bags very quickly.

Your business practices must be up to par. Your quality has to be on point. You have got to separate your company from the many other lines on the market. Many designers think that you achieve this through creating different designs. The way you run your business is just as important as your designs. You have to be firm in your beliefs and terms. A compromise here and there may be necessary but don't make it a norm if it will jeopardize your company.

Magic Tradeshow

Dealing with retailers at tradeshows like the Magic is tricky. As we told you in our other two books, most new lines are desperate to get orders. In reality, you should be concerned with who you sell your brand to. You don't want someone posing to have a store who is really selling out of her basement or trunk.

Larger clothing companies require buyers to present a certain amount of information to be able to even see the line let alone carry them. Non-Desperate brands strictly enforce many of the following requirements:

- Store has been in business for at least one year

- Require a financial statement

- Must be approved by the factor if they don't do COD

- Must have pictures of their store inside and out

- Must carry other similar brands in their store

- Can't carry knock-offs

- May send a representative to inspect the store

- Must order certain minimums

- Must be a certain distance from another retailer selling their clothing already

- Require a deposit down to open the account

Desperate new lines at Magic don't care about half of these things. They will write up and order for anybody that wants to write. Many times they end up with bogus orders because of this. Just as there are many want-to-be clothing lines, there are want-to-be retailers. It must be one of your practices to require each new account to put down a shipping deposit.

Make sure you save each stores shipping deposit. Then every time you ship an order to that particular store, let them still pay for the shipping with each incoming order. Then, if a time ever arises where they don't accept their order, you can then deduct the shipping charges from their deposit. This way you will never get stuck holding the shipping bag. You would be surprised at how many stores order items that they don't accept once the items reach their door.

To a certain extent, taking deposits at Magic also locks a retailer into carrying your line. Deposits also show you that a retailer is serious. The key thing in this is that you only want to use their deposit money for it was intended. If a store decides they don't want to work with you and want their deposit back, you should have it available to give to them minus any shipping fees charged to them.

You will get many valuable contacts from the Magic TradeShow such as manufacturers, factors, and models. The models come in handy sometimes when you may need one of them to start working for you on the spot.

Another aspect of Magic is about how much you should be spending. Many new companies go to Magic and overspend easily. I recall our second time going to Magic. We decided to take eight models from our home city, plus our sales staff and company owners. We paid for the models' hotel rooms, plane tickets and daily expenses.

There is an agency that works with Magic that can supply you with models, but they can be rather expensive. Usually, there are plenty of models just walking around who will model for your company on the spot if you pay them. The other thing you can do is to use mannequins. We found that a mix of mannequins and real models was the best selling mechanism.

The last thing to mention about Magic is that your booth location is everything. You want to be located in main aisles where there is a lot of foot traffic. You also want to be located next to other hot brands. The best way to ensure you get a good location is to tell Magic organizers who you would like to be next to. The other thing is you have to pay them as early as possible as prime booth spaces generally go to those who pay first.

Sales Representatives

Sales Reps are an important part of your business. You cannot be everywhere at one time, so you need people out there whose only concern is to sell your clothing. Many new designers turn to reps who are selling for other lines to help get them in the door in many places. These types of reps are expensive as we mentioned in our other two books.

Industry sales reps don't take on new lines for the most part. Reps selling to retailers, who have trust in them, is their bread and butter. If they sell your unproven line in all of their retail connections and you don't come through, it will damage their credibility. Their credibly is far more important to them than picking up your line, even if you have a hot design.

We hear reps talk all the time about this company and that company. It is quite interesting hearing about the business through the eyes of a clothing rep. They have their own ideas as to how to be successful in this industry. We have had the pleasure to experience life from all points of view, which is what makes us experts on this subject.

One rep told us how he sold a new line to all of these retailers and the clothing company could not deliver. The orders were late, and sometimes they didn't come at all. This line had a celebrity face to it, which is why the rep took the line in the first place. The rep lost a few of his key accounts because he carried a line that didn't perform. Stores hold grudges when they lose money.

In our beginnings, we approached a rep who was writing millions of dollars in orders for a major label. He was very impressed with our designs. He felt we were very original and would go far in the business. He said that he would not even consider representing our line until we had three successful seasons of on-time shipping, quality products, and in-your-face advertising under our belt.

He said he would check with our retailers to see how we were doing with those things. Another rep was only concerned with how much extensive advertising we would be doing. He wanted to see our financial statements and our design forecast. Reps don't play around when it comes to picking up a new line.

There are others who will say they'll take your line on for a certain price. They may carry your line along with them but may not push your line as much as their other lines. In order for your sales rep to push your line, you have to be positioned right as we mentioned earlier. If your line is weak in terms of lack of demand, no one will respect it, even if you are paying them. Of course you can follow the advice we mentioned in volume I on getting a rep; that may prove beneficial to you. Even with that approach, you still need a hot line to truly jump off in the retail world.

Another aspect of the sales rep segment of your company is fair treatment. We have heard countless stories of reps leaving a company because they felt unappreciated. A good rep should make good money. It is that simple. If you do not pay your reps for a good performance, the next guy will.

You also have to make sure that you are paying your rep's commission off the top. As human beings, we tend to want to do things by the book, but in reality often waiver. Say you just cashed a check for $5,000. Your rep's commission is $1,000 of that amount. Your rent at your warehouse is due and for this example say it is $5,000. You aren't expecting any extra cash into your company for three and a half more weeks.
The warehouse rental office will not tolerate any more late payments from you. Many companies have chosen to pay the rent

first. What if you make this decision and in three and a half weeks you don't get the amount of money you were planning on. There are reps who have left companies because the company owes them a considerable amount of money. You have to take care of your sales team. Make sure that you figure their commissions properly. You don't want to short them, or overpay them for that matter.

Being a traveling sales rep is a hard job. Traveling reps are away from their families selling your product. They have to believe in your product to be good at selling your product. If they sense a weakness on the end of your company, it will reflect in their presentation. If they are carrying more than one line, they may end up not showing yours at all to a buyer. Good sales people can get your business off to a great start providing you have all of your business in order.

There are reps who can become your company's nightmare as well. These reps will take your company to the bank without producing a dime in sales. We had one rep who wrote only one order in his whole three-month stay with us. Get this. The one order he wrote turned out to be a bogus order from his brother who had a fake store. His credentials had checked out but I guess we didn't investigate him thoroughly enough. In this business, make it a

point to investigate to the utmost anyone or any company you
will be doing business with. Don't just trust them on the
strength of what they are saying.

We told this rep that we would cover his daily expenses at Magic
Tradeshow only if he produced sales. He had this big book of
retailers that he was saying he invited to come to our booth.
None of his so-called appointments showed up that week. He
blamed it on our booth location.

The bottom line is he was a joke and we fired him right there at
Magic. We wanted him to return our samples to us after the show.
Therefore, what he did was send them to us COD for the $700 he
claimed we owed him from coming to Magic. Needless to say, he
became the proud owner of those samples.

In closing, make sure you and your sales team are prepared when
dealing with retailers big and small. From our sales guide,
which gives you the basics, to this book, which gives you the
behind the scenes footage, you should be ready to tackle this
task. Remember, retailers are the lifeline of your company.
Their success or failure is your success or failure.

Opening Your Own Store(s)

Having your own store is expensive but may be necessary. A prime example of why owning your own store may become inevitable is the experience of Tommy Hilfiger in 2004. Tommy Hilfiger opened twenty-nine new stores in 2004. While their wholesale profits were down in 2004, their sales direct from their own stores were showing great numbers.

Opening your own store – or stores - allows you to be less dependent upon other retailers. Many designers have found opening their own store to be truly beneficial and rewarding. The bottom line is this. When you sell directly to the consumer, you will make four times your investment. For example:

- Say you paid $10 for something.

- You wholesale it for $20.

- The store then sells it to their customer for $42.

- You too would be selling your clothing for $42 from your own store.

- You will make $32 on the sale while the retail store only makes $22.

If you sell half the amount of your produced goods from your store and half from retailers, you can expect to have higher profits. It is because of this that you may be able to sell your product for less than you really want or need just to make sure your wholesale prices are market friendly.

You definitely want to sell your merchandise for the price you are requiring other retailers to. If you don't, they will not carry your line. Why would customers buy it from them when they can get it from you cheaper? In addition, you should open an internet store without even thinking twice about it. We have sold to customers from all over the world from our website. Note, however, that internet sales cannot solely support your company. Look at internet sales as a supplement.

Competition

No matter how you look at it, you are competing with other clothing lines. You may think you have no competition because you have the hottest designs out, but that will not be the case. You are competing for your brand's place in the mind of the consumer. You are competing with other lines for a piece of your retailer's budget. You will have to earn your success, beyond just producing a hot design.

Advertising, Sales and Marketing

Until you are a famous brand, the primary goal of your advertising should be to make money. Establishing brand awareness remains secondary. For the most part your advertising should channel consumers to a certain product you are selling. The key theme of your advertising is a product you are actually selling.

You do not want to advertise something that the people cannot buy. This will not help your bottom line or make your precious advertising dollars make sense. Don't be scared to call off an ad or push it back if your product is delayed or canceled. You also want to make sure you are advertising thru companies that are connecting with your target market. There are plenty of places to advertise so make sure you choose them wisely.

Being a new clothing company, you are sometimes faced with a dilemma. Should you concentrate your advertising and marketing efforts regionally or nationally? Regionally is a great idea if you didn't have other factors to consider. The primary determining factor for aiming regionally or nationally is, usually, how much product **you have to order** from the factory.

The more accounts you have, the better your chances will be of selling out. You can't control where people like your product. You may find that your retailers are spread out all over the country. Your advertising efforts would have to aim nationally in this case. This doesn't mean you shouldn't engage in some locally driven promotions where your accounts are located.

When you mention the word national there is a cost involved. With that in mind, don't spend too many dollars on local advertising that is too expensive. We have seen some locally produced magazines that cost almost as much as some national publications. You will have to figure out the most cost efficient way for you to reach your target market.

Remember this story as well. There was a company that started out after we did. They advertised in all of the major magazines for eight months before they even brought their first product out. What new designers don't realize is that your first ads are the most important. People are drawn to new lines. They want to be the first to sell or wear it, especially after seeing advertisements for the new line. However, they will want exactly what they see in the ad.

In our very first national ad, we didn't have anything in the ad in production or in our warehouse. We got an overwhelming amount of calls for our ad items, which we had printed up for image branding with no real intention to sell. This was a huge mistake. As you know now, the amount of time it takes to get your product made and to the stores is pretty long. By the time we thought about actually producing the styles we had advertised, the buzz that the ads had generated was gone. Let the big guys build image and brand awareness. You focus on selling your product. Remember this advice: **a print ad is like a catalog page with a message.**

Back to the clothing company we mentioned that did a vast amount of advertising before their line even came out. They advertised like crazy all over the place. Most of their advertising didn't make sense however. There were times when the owner of the line even had himself in the pictures with the other models. What were they selling? Another thing to note is the fact that they went out of business owing a lot of money to various magazines who had given them credit.

This is why we warned in Volume 1 to accept credit with caution. Make sure you get the most out of your advertising dollars. We have cancelled free ads just because a product we wanted to advertise was going to be late. Don't take credit terms on an ad thinking you will be able to sell enough merchandise from the hype of the ad to cover the cost.

Now the line we mentioned actually got picked up in over 200 stores based on their advertising. They did well in half of their accounts, while the other half struggled to sell their product. Their catalog of unfocused ads had failed to generate the demand in their target market that would lead them into supporting the line. Many stores stopped ordering from them. Others didn't pay their outstanding invoices with them. The retail backlash from their clothing not selling well ended their business. Advertising alone can only get you so far.

Participating In Someone Else's Fashion Show: to do or not to do?

Fashion shows - a night of glamour or a waste of money. In this section we'll examine both scenarios to present you with the proper insight into the world of catwalks, models, and so-called exposure. A fashion show is a collection of designers showcasing their designs for the upcoming season.

Traditionally, the designers are not charged a fee for their participation in these shows; however, these designers are well known to attract public interest. In your local area, there may be a fee for you to exhibit your line in a show; however, you should use good judgment when deciding which shows to participate in. In retrospect, it's safe to say that we misapplied a sizeable amount of dollars on the runway. Fortunately, for you these manuals have been written to stop you from making similar mistakes. Lucky you!

Ok, quick question, if an invitation is extended to you to showcase your clothing line in a fashion show, should you have to pay? Well it depends on many factors. Below we name a few:

- Who are the main attractions featured in the show?

- Are there any fees involved?

- By participating, will your sales increase?

- Will you gain real exposure for your line?

- How much advertising and marketing will be done for the show?

- Will your line be mentioned in the advertising of the show?

These are some of the things to consider when you are thinking about participating in a fashion show.

The main objective for being in business is to make money. If a promoter wants you to pay a fee to partake in his fashion show, you might want to consider not doing it, unless your line stands to really benefit. For example, if a fashion show is going to be held in your local area with established brands showcasing their lines for the upcoming season, you might want to be involved, even if there is a fee.

The reason why is because by placing your line among well-known brands you give off the image of stability while promoting brand awareness. Now here is where things get tricky. The fee could cost you anywhere from $1,000 to $2,500. You will have to decide if your company will benefit from exhibiting at such a fashion show. In my opinion, you might want to participate once or twice for the experience and opportunity to present your line with the big boys. This could also be good for your brand's image!

Ok, have you heard the old saying "if it doesn't make dollars, it doesn't make (cents) sense?" Well, that's not just a cliché, in business it is a fact. When it comes to doing fashion shows, you have to be careful not to channel too much of your investment funds in that direction. In life we are all in search of balance, balance of our families, careers, love life, and spirituality. Why should the fashion industry be exempt from that divine process?

The point I'm making here is when you pour your hard earned money into some other person's venture, be sure that it's going to balance out for your benefit. Therefore, in conclusion, our team learned to intelligently appropriate our dollars. Instead of a fashion show to gain exposure, we started investing in the service of public relation firms or other more efficient means to gain better exposure.

The proper channeling of funds is critical in the beginning stages of your company. Be careful not to spend too much money

on fashion shows. At best, a fashion show provides only one
night of glamour then its' back to the real world.

Photo Shoots

Another aspect of creating your advertising and marketing
campaign stems from great **photo shoots**. A good photo shoot is
the result of a well-planned storyboard to convey your company's
message.

In our beginning stages, we had some quite interesting photo
shoots. One of our first photo shoots was for a national
magazine. We were very excited. We had a few models show up for
the shoot along with make-up people, a stylist and a few
spectators. We were doing the photo shoot inside of the
photographer's studio. It was our first experience with a photo
shoot, so things were quite interesting.

The male models were too busy flirting with the female models.
Some of the female models had brought their boyfriends, who
didn't want their girlfriends posing certain ways. The make-up
artist made up one person in a way we didn't like. The
photographer didn't really have a good vision of what to do. The

experience became somewhat chaotic. Yet all of these things were our fault and could have been avoided with proper planning.

Some good photo's came out of the shoot. We would have hoped so after spending a total of $2,000 on the photo shoot, which is cheap by many standards. A top-notch photographer can cost you that amount alone. Remember the best photographers do cost money and you get what you pay for. Just to let you know as well, we had used a mixture of professional models and amateurs in this shoot.

What exactly is a professional model? A professional model is someone who has been trained to model and has modeling experience. To have a successful photo shoot there are certain things that must be adhered to. Sure, photo shoots should be fun but there is a limit to the play. If you are doing a photo shoot, you should make sure of the following:

- No boyfriends, girlfriends, or friends of any kind on the set
- All models must arrive on time or be docked, or not used
- All models and photographers must sign releases
- Keep other spectators off of the set (even your own friends)

- Give the make-up people a clear description of how to make up each person

- Don't be afraid to tell the make-up artist to redo someone's makeup if you aren't satisfied

- Make sure the clothes you are taking are in good condition

- Make sure you have a clear idea of the kind of shots you need for your campaign, e.g., a well planned storyboard

- Make sure your photographer is using good film

- Make sure you or anyone else isn't flirting with the models

- Keep things professional during the shoot

- Male and female models aren't allowed to trade phone numbers during the photo shoot

- Everyone knows in advance what they are getting paid

- Everyone has a clear idea on how you will use the pictures

- Models know that you may or may not use their picture after the shoot

- Models should be told in advance if you want them to bring or wear anything special to the shoot.

Doing the above things can lead to a successful photo shoot, which can lead to a great advertising campaign.

Public Relations - Your PR Strategy

The very best thing for your line will be hiring a PR firm. A good public relations strategy is very important to the new clothing line. PR. Take a good look at those two letters because you are going to want and need to see more of them. PR is going to be more of a friend to you than advertising will ever be. Why? Because it can serve you well? Advertising is what you are trying to say about yourself; PR is what others are saying about you. For example, if you tell someone that you make the best chicken in town, they may or may not believe you.

Now imagine if a third party told someone that you make the best chicken in town. That person would be more likely to believe a third party rather than hearing the same from you. This is called third party confirmation. What others are saying about you carries more weight than what you say about yourself. In reference to your clothing line, get others to talk about your garments, and the public will believe it! That is what PR is all about.

It will be up to you to decide what message your line will convey. What is the content of your line? What is the definition that will define the meaning of your line? How will you be different or separate from others? These are questions that only you can answer, and whatever those answers are, PR will be the best medium to speak to the consumer with. In closing, publicity can be free or it will come with a price. You can save money by doing the legwork yourself or hire a firm to develop a PR campaign for you.

The Cash Flow of a Clothing Company

Here again is a graph of the typical cash flow period based on each phase from ordering your product to actually receiving it.

Cash Flow In the Apparel Industry by Average Number of Days.

Start Order Downpayment	Finish Production Pay Balance	Ship Goods Air	Ship Goods Ocean	Clear Customs	Time to ship goods into your warehouse	You ship to Retailers	COD delivery to you	Bank Clear Money Order
	60	7	40	4	1	5	7	5

Total Time by Air:		89						
Total Time by Ocean:		122						

In the above example, you see that the total number of days from putting a down payment on your order to actually having funds available in your bank account from selling the order is around 122 (ocean shipping).

Another thing to keep in mind is that sometimes shipments are late, as we mentioned, which could add ten to twenty days more on top of this. Our current record for the latest production order was 120 days. This is standard for some larger manufacturers, but not for us. There is always the potential for things to go wrong somewhere in this timeline.

Many times retailers will ask you to ship their goods on a certain day, which may be a few days after you get the orders. You are ready to ship them as soon as you get them to start making money. Then you have the retailers that you ship to that don't pay the COD when the order gets there.

You have all of these potential delays at your door. The other side of this is the excess inventory you ordered that has not been ordered yet by your retailers yet. You will be trying to find retail homes for those excess items. All these things have the potential to push back your income on this order. You can go from 122 days reaping the financial benefits of the order to 152 days or more easily.

This is why we told you in the beginning that securing your pipeline is critical. If you were to do one big order and then try to fund future orders off the big order, you would not be ordering your new product for at least 140 days. Then it would be another 140 days or so before you earn money off that order. You have basically wasted a whole year on two orders if this is your plan.

The toughest part of your clothing business will be getting your pipeline and cash flow to run like a well-oiled machine. It is in this stage that the most capital is needed. Once you have your cash flow turning, you just have to make sure your product is selling.

Many designers plan what they will bring out by what they want to see come out in a particular season. This is fine to do. The ultimate approval will be made by your budget, however. The budget may say you can only do three styles instead of the seven that you wanted to.

At the end of every month, you want to make sure you have a positive cash flow. Adding on styles to any given month will depend on your available cash. A successful clothing line should always have a healthy cash flow at the end of every month. You never want to have your budget so tight that if things go wrong you get in financial trouble. In terms of forecasting on your income statement, you will have to be realistic. Donald Trump once said that even the best laid plans don't always go accordingly.

If your cash flow at the end of a month is negative, you will have to backtrack through your pipeline and either raise prices, trim expenses, adjust quantities or cut styles. This may also be a sign that you are trying to do too much. The larger your cash flow is at the end of the month the better. It will shield your company from slow sales and other difficulties that may arise.

Your basic income statement (used for projections) should include these items:

Month

- **Sales Income**

    Direct Sales via your website and/or store

    Wholesales segment direct by you

    Wholesale segment by sales reps (subject to commission)

- Cost of Goods Sold (includes)

    Down payment on next order

    Balance to be paid on your incoming order

    Shipping Cost of your incoming order

    Estimated Duty cost of incoming order

- Gross Net Profit

- Total Expenses

    Advertising

    Sales Rep Commission

    Website

    Loans

    Employees/Salaries

    Supplies

    Samples

    Shipping and Mailing

    Rent

Utilities

- Net Income for the month

- Cash Flow Balance + / - at the end of the month

Your beginning cash flow at the beginning of the month is whatever you had left over from the previous month. To get your new balance, you add your net profit or loss from the current month to the cash flow.

Your cash flow is the most important aspect of your company. It ties right in with your pipeline. If your pipeline struggles and you fail to add to your cash flow every month, your cash flow will start to dwindle. This will make it hard for you to keep your projected pace. You may find yourself having to borrow money to keep things going as you would like. Borrowing will not ultimately solve your problem. Your problem is that your sales are not being generated to the extent that you need.

If you do not correct the problem you will find yourself in debt. The bottom line is you have to sell whatever you order. You have to be profitable to stay alive. Your goal should be to sell out of every order in thirty days or less. To do this you will need to have your incoming order already pre-sold.

Do not get caught up in the belief that you can borrow your way through anything. Borrowing is a temporary fix. There will come a day when you can't borrow any more. Do not let your company get in this position. This is why we advocate that you have a strong sales plan and well-forecasted pipeline.

Sometimes you don't know what will be a hit with consumers and what will not, and retailers can be fickle. Your business is at the mercy of other people. You are depending on your supplier to ship on time. You are depending on them to ship you quality. You are depending on retailers to order your products. You are depending on consumers to support your products.

I want to touch on another quick subject just for your reference. When you are planning your pipeline, you will want to be somewhat lean on your January and June delivery months. These are slow months in this industry. There is not a lot of wholesale buying going on, so you don't want to order too much merchandise in these months or you may not be able to sell it all within thirty days.

Please understand that you have to perform. You may have looked at your company as a design company. That is the wrong outlook. Instead, think of yourself as a Fortune 500 company. You have to perform financially to stay afloat. You will have to make key financial decisions to make sure your business will be able to grow and expand. Just as many companies have gone out of business because they aren't selling; there are those that fold because they mistakenly tried to accommodate a huge demand.

If you can't service all of your accounts, then you should raise your retail order minimums and cut the weaker stores. It really makes no sense to go out of business trying to do something you probably can't do anyway. Say that overnight you find yourself with a $1,000,000 in orders for one month's release. To produce the goods to support $1,000,000 in sales may cost you around $500,000.

Say you only have $200,000 available in your pipeline to cover four months of releases. This would break down to $50,000 a month. You are $450,000 short of being able to meet the $1,000,000 demand. Don't do what others have done. Don't take your whole $200,000 and let it ride on this one big order. We talked about this in the beginning of this book in the pipeline section. Be modest and take things slowly.

You are the master of your clothing company. You alone dictate what you do. There is no law that states you have to service all of those orders if you can't do it in a healthy way. If you have a large investor who wants to back these orders, then go for it. If you don't, you will have to go to a select distribution channel. Only the hottest stores, which are ordering the most, will have your products.

You can add on stores as your cash flow grows. It is that simple. Sure you will lose some of the stores that wanted to order your goods. They may get mad and never want to order from you again. Which would you rather have — a few stores mad at you or your company going out of business? The fact remains that for those who take this risk, putting all of their money on the big order, will find themselves caught up. This has happened to a large brand that we know of. The brand was sold everywhere as there was a significant demand for it but is now out of business.

You have to pace yourself correctly and let your business grow. Do not be afraid to turn down orders. You have to be smart. Are you just here to be a one hit wonder or are you here to have long-term success? You will have to be the one to decide.

Clothing Industry Myths

To succeed in this business you first have to get some myths out of your head. The top ten clothing industry myths are:

1. Finding a manufacturer automatically means you will succeed.

2. Banks will loan you money just because you have a great business plan and orders.

3. A larger company will come to your rescue and offer you a distribution deal.

4. A good name automatically means success.

5. Having a booth at Magic guarantees that the buyers will come to your booth to order.

6. Advertising automatically translate into sales.

7. Celebrity endorsements automatically bring you sales.

8. Most manufacturers do quality work.

9. A production deal will present itself if you get many orders.

10. Having a lot of money behind you guarantees success.

The Top 12 Factors that Determine Success

1. Efficient use of financial assets and planning

2. Selling out of each order within thirty days at least 85 percent of the time

3. Quality Manufacturing and Merchandise

4. On time shipping of a well-planned pipeline

5. Support from retailers and consumers

6. A great pricing structure on your products

7. A strong team dedicated to the success of the company

8. Hot designs

9. A good image and brand awareness

10. A great advertising and public relations plan

11. Great customer service

12. A fantastic name

Successful lines are the ones that adapt to changes in the environment. At times you will have to reinvent your company to stay fresh in the consumer's mind. You have to think like a champion. You cannot underestimate your competition. You have to be able to think outside of the box and come up with creative ways to move your company forward.

What worked for another company may not work for your company. Fubu was able to achieve success due to the use of LL Cool J, but for the most part this is not reality any more for upcoming lines. There are exceptions of course, but they are few.

You have to be quick on your feet to overcome obstacles. You must think with a business mind instead of a designer's mind. Having a clothing company is a business while being a designer is a skill and a gift. Just because you are a designer doesn't make you a good businessperson. This book helps you make that leap - from designer to being a great designer and businessperson. Just think, can a trained doctor necessarily possess the expertise to start and operate a whole hospital?

There are days when you may fail at something. You have to get right back up and keep running the race to make your company successful.

With All of These Potential Problems – Why Do We Do It?

The apparel industry is a ninety billion dollar per year problematic industry. Things are always going wrong. The days where things go according to plan are very limited. Yet it is those days that make everything worthwhile. There is nothing quite like selling out of an order and having stores call us to order more.

There have been few things more satisfying than seeing samples come in for the first time and having them be a true reflection of our vision. We still get excited whenever we see other people wear our clothes no matter who they are. We love when a customer calls in and tells us how much they love our clothes they just ordered.

We love seeing our clothes come down the runway and hearing people clapping and congratulating us. Photo shoots and ads coming alive are awesome. Traveling and meeting new people all around the world are beautiful things. We love seeing the write-ups on our garments in magazines.

The personal financial benefits you can reap from running a successful clothing line can be substantial. The status, fame and recognition you may receive from having a hot line will make you proud. There is no feeling better than people appreciating you for your creativity. This is why we do what we do. These will become your reasons for persevering as well.

When the good things happen, it makes all of the sleepless nights worthwhile. It is this passion that keeps us going even in the midst of darkness. Let this book help you on your path. Formulate your own plan of action using this book as a general outline for success. We wish you the very best in your endeavors.

Good Luck and God Bless!